YOUR KNOWLEDGE HAS VALUE

AF151973

- We will publish your bachelor's and
  master's thesis, essays and papers

- Your own eBook and book -
  sold worldwide in all relevant shops

- Earn money with each sale

Upload your text at www.GRIN.com
and publish for free

Bibliographic information published by the German National Library:

The German National Library lists this publication in the National Bibliography; detailed bibliographic data are available on the Internet at http://dnb.dnb.de .

This book is copyright material and must not be copied, reproduced, transferred, distributed, leased, licensed or publicly performed or used in any way except as specifically permitted in writing by the publishers, as allowed under the terms and conditions under which it was purchased or as strictly permitted by applicable copyright law. Any unauthorized distribution or use of this text may be a direct infringement of the author s and publisher s rights and those responsible may be liable in law accordingly.

Imprint:

Copyright © 2015 GRIN Verlag, Open Publishing GmbH
Print and binding: Books on Demand GmbH, Norderstedt Germany
ISBN: 978-3-668-05526-1

This book at GRIN:

http://www.grin.com/en/e-book/306022/overview-of-germany-s-social-security-system-principles-and-historical

Andreas Manthey

Overview of Germany's Social Security System. Principles and Historical Development

GRIN Publishing

GRIN - Your knowledge has value

Since its foundation in 1998, GRIN has specialized in publishing academic texts by students, college teachers and other academics as e-book and printed book. The website www.grin.com is an ideal platform for presenting term papers, final papers, scientific essays, dissertations and specialist books.

Visit us on the internet:

http://www.grin.com/

http://www.facebook.com/grincom

http://www.twitter.com/grin_com

WE TALK ABOUT:

S O C I A L   S E C U R I T Y

S Y S T E M

I.Social State Principle,

main features of the social security

1.
THE WELFARE STATE

1.1
HISTORICAL DEVELOPMENT
OF THE SOCIAL SYSTEM

Precursor in antiquity, Middle Ages and modern times

15 Century

- TILL 15 CENT. NO REGULATIONS
- FAMILY
- WITH PROPAGATION OF THE CHRISTIANITY: CHURCHES, CLOISTERS
- WITH STRONGER GROWING TOWNS: GUILDS

18 Century

- EXAMPLE PRUSSIA: ESTABLISHMENT POORHOUSES, COMMUNITY HOMES FOR YOUNGSTERS
- POOR RELIEF, MINE-EMPLOYEES: SOCIAL MINERS

19 Century

- STATE HAS RECOGNISED HIS SOCIAL RESPONSIBILITY, THE FIRST LEGISLATIONS WITH FAR-REACHING CONSEQUENCES, **THEREFORE**:

„IMPERIAL MESSAGE"
(KAISERLICHE BOTSCHAFT)
OF NOVEMBER 17th, 1881
Source: http://germanhistorydocs.ghi-dc.org/images/30003151-p1.jpg

(ANNOUNCEMENT OF A LAW OF THE PROTECTION OF THE WORKERS WITH ACCIDENT, ILLNESS AND AGE AND OTHER SOCIAL LAWS)

SOCIAL LEGISLATION

[IMPERIAL CHANCELLOR: OTTO VON BISMARCK]

- WAS NEW FOR THE WORLD AT THIS TIME
  AND GROUNDBREAKING

- STILL TODAY LAID THE FOUNDATION-STONE FOR
  OURS FUNCTIONING SOCIAL SYSTEM OF GERMANY

SOCIAL LEGISLATION – TIME LINE

1881
ANNOUNCEMENT (IMPERIAL MESSAGE)

1883
INTRODUCTION HEALTH INSURANCE LAW
(IMPERIAL ASSURANCE ORDER - RVO)

1884
INTRODUCTION ACCIDENT INSURANCE LAW
(IMPERIAL ASSURANCE ORDER – ENLARGEMENT RVO)

1889
INTRODUCTION LAW ABOUT OCCUPATIONAL DISABILITY
 AND RETIREMENT PENSION INSURANCE
(IMPERIAL ASSURANCE ORDER – ENLARGEMENT RVO)

SOCIAL LEGISLATION – TIME LINE

1927
LAW ABOUT EMPLOYMENT-FINDING AND UNEMPLOYMENT

...

1953
SOCIAL COURT LAW

1957/1963
REFORM OF OLD AGE PENSION SCHEME AND LEGAL ACCIDENT INSURANCE

SOCIAL LEGISLATION – TIME LINE

1962
INTRODUCTION FEDERAL SOCIAL ASSISTANCE ACT
FOR THE FIRST TIME: LEGAL ENTITLEMENT TO CARE OF THE STATE (LEAST CARE); BEFORE ADMINISTRATIVE DISCRETION

1974/75
INSURANCE OF REHABILITATION AND HANDICAPPED PEOPLE

...

TRANSFORMATION DIFFERENT SOCIAL ORDERS
IN SOCIAL CODES (SGB PART 1 TO 12)

SOCIAL LEGISLATION – TIME LINE

1995
INTRODUCTION OF COMPULSORY LONG TERM CARE INSURANCE
(NURSING INSURANCE)

..CURRENT:
DIFFERENT REFORM ACTS

1.2

THE SOCIAL STATE PRINCIPLE

WHAT IT MEANS:

SOCIAL STATE PRINCIPLE ?

SOCIAL STATE PRINCIPLE

OBJECTIVE:

THE STATE HAS OBLIGATION OF,

-**EXISTENCE PRECAUTION**
-**PREVENTION OF MATERIAL NEED AND SOCIAL DESCENT**
-**SECURITY OF LIFE RISKS**

FOR THE PROTECTION OF THE SOCIAL PEACE
(**SOCIAL JUSTICE**)

SOCIAL STATE PRINCIPLE

... IS NOT A STIFF PRINCIPLE, BUT HAS TO GO ON NEWS
DEVELOPMENTS CAN REACT ...

... THE ARRANGEMENT OF THE PRINCIPLE BECAME BY THEM
FATHERS OF THE BASIC LAW TO THE LEGISLATOR
LEAVE ...

LANDMARK:
JUDGMENT OF THE FEDERAL CONSTITUTIONAL COURT
(From June 24, 1954)
→ FOR THE FIRST TIME LEGAL ENTITLEMENT TO PUBLIC CARE

WHY WE TALK
GENERALLY ABOUT
SOCIAL AFFAIRS?

BASIC LAW OF GERMANY
(CONSTITUNIONAL LAW)

FEDERAL REPUBLIC OF GERMANY

HAS CONFESSED TO THE SOCIAL STATE PRINCIPLE
AND HAS ESTABLISHED IN THE BASIC LAW.
→ ANCHORAGE SOCIAL STATE ORDER

THEREFORE:
THE STATE HAS THE OBJECTIVE AND OBLIGATION FOR
THE CITIZENS!

BASIC LAW OF GERMANY

ARTICEL 1
UNTOUCHABILITY OF THE HUMAN DIGNITY

PARAGRAPH 1:
THE DIGNITY OF THE HUMANS IS UNTOUCHABLE. TO RESPECT
THEM AND TO PROTECTION IS OBLIGATION OF ALL STATE
POWER.

ARTICEL 20
THE FEDERAL REPUBLIC IS A DEMOCRATIC AND SOCIAL
FEDERAL STATE.

Supplement of the Social State Principle by
Fundamental rights (Basic Law)

ARTICLE 6, PARAGRAPH 1
PROTECTION OF MARRIAGE AND FAMILY

ARTICLE 6, PARAGRAPH 4
MATERNITY PROTECTION

ARTICLE 12
OCCUPATIONAL FREEDOM, FORBADE FROM HARD LABOUR

ARTICLE 14
PROPERTY OBLIGES

Fundamental rights

... ARE FOR ALL STATE FACILITIES
OBLIGATORILY AND VALID RIGHT!

→THEREFORE THE „JOB" OF THE STATE!
THE LEGISLATION, MANAGEMENT AND ADMINISTRATION OF
JUSTICE HAS THE OBLIGATION TO AN ACTIVE CO_AUTHORED
THE SOCIAL JUSTICE AND SOCIAL BALANCE

TIP:
FROM IT RESULTED NO INDIVIDUAL CLAIM ON
CERTAIN ACHIEVEMENTS, BUT ONLY BY
LEGISLATION, E.G., SOCIAL LAW BOOK

BUT:

SOCIAL STATE LEADS NOT TO THE COMPLETE "WELFARE STATE", BUT THE CITIZEN HAS

OWN RESPONSIBILITY / OBLIGATION TO THE SELF-HELP
OBLIGATIONS OPPONENT TO THE STATE
(E.G., SOCIAL COMPULSORY INSURANCE, TAX DUTY)

ONE CALLS COMBINATION OF SOCIAL AND JURIDICAL DEFAULT
AND THE OBLIGATIONS OF THE CITIZENS
SOCIAL CONSTITUTIONAL STATE

ROLE OF THE STATE

•DEFINITIONS OF THE LEGAL BASIC CONDITIONS.
  E.G., SOCIAL CODES (SGB)

•THE LEGISLATIVE INTERVENE WITH ECONOMIC AND
SOCIAL SKEW SITUATION
  E.G., TOPICAL DISCUSSION FOR THE ADAPTATION „HARTZ
  CONTROL SENTENCES IV" (Basic benefits in case of unemployment)

Social constitutional state (compactly)

SOCIAL STATE

- •SOCIAL BALANCE
- •SOCIALJUSTICE
- •HUMAN DIGNITY
- •WELFARE OF ALL HUMANS

CONSTITUTIONAL STATE

- •LEGITIMACY OF THE STATE MANAGEMENT
- •CONNECTION OF THE STATE POWER TO FUNDAMENTAL RIGHTS
- • PROTECTION OF SINGLE HUMAN

SOCIAL CONSTITUTIONAL STATE

- •SOCIAL RIGHTS OF THE SINGLE HUMAN
- •SOCIAL DUTIES OF THE SINGLE HUMAN
- •JUSTICE AND LEGALITY
- •PROTECTION AND PROSPERITY

1.3
GUARANTEED CONTINUANCE

WHAT IT MEANS:
<u>GUARANTEED CONTINUANCE</u> ?

<u>GUARANTEED CONTINUANCE</u>

<u>CONSTITUTIONAL-JURIDICAL BASIC DECISIONS</u>

- **SOCIAL STATE**

- **CONSTITUTIONAL STATE**

- **FEDERAL STATE** (ARTIKEL 28 BASIC LAW)

- **DEMOCRACY** (ALL AUTHORITY OF THE STATE GOES OUT FROM THE PEOPLE, RULE ON TIME)

- **REPUBLIC** (FORM OF GOVERNMENT, FEDERAL PRESIDENT AS THE HEAD OF STATE)

→ <u>"ETERNITY CLAUSE"</u>←
(ARTICEL 79 PARAGRAPH 3 BASIC LAW)

GUARANTEED CONTINUANCE

OBJECTIVE:

NO ONE / NONE SHOULD HAVE THE POSSIBILITY IN THE
PARLIAMENT TO CHANGE THESE REGULATIONS.

CONSEQUENCE:
ALL FUNDAMENTAL RIGHTS STAND UNDER THE SPECIAL
PROTECTION OF THE CONTINUANCE GUARANTEE

GUARANTEED CONTINUANCE

OBLIGATION OF THE FEDERAL STATES

ARTICEL 28 PARAGRAPH 1 BASIC LAW
SAYS THAT THE ORDER ACCORDING TO CONSTITUTION ALL
STATES OF GERMANY MUST CORRESPOND TO THE PRINCIPLES
OF THE REPUBLICAN, DEMOCRATIC AND SOCIAL OF
CONSTITUTIONAL STATE.

EXAMPLE, STATE OF BERLIN:
ARTICLE 22 PARAGRAPH 1 OF THE CONSTITUTION
… TO REALISE OBLIGATION OF THE COUNTRY WITHIN THE SCOPE
OF HIS FORCES THE SOCIAL PROTECTION …

2.

THE SYSTEM
OF THE SOCIAL
SECURITY IN GERMANY

2.1

THE SOCIAL NET
OF THE FEDERAL REPUBLIC
OF GERMANY

WHAT IS YOUR UNDERSTANDING OF

„**SOCIAL NET**" AND

WHICH <u>SOCIAL BENEFITS</u> YOU KNOW?

SOCIAL NET IS THE SUM OF ALL SOCIAL BENEFITS OF THE (FEDERAL) STATE.

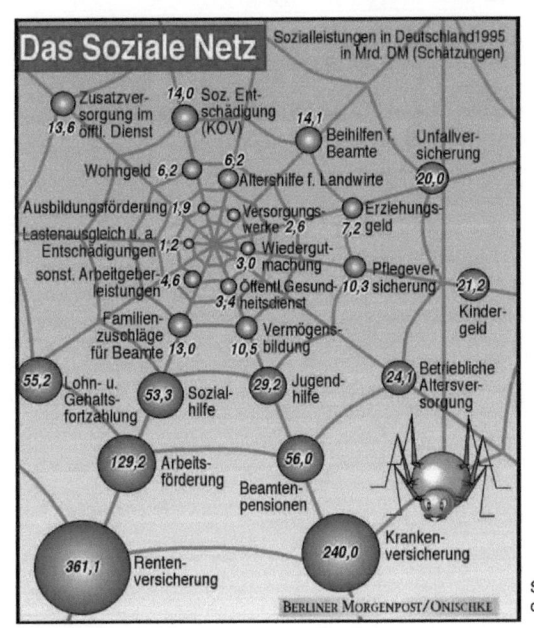

SOCIAL BENEFITS

Source: http://www.kreativ-onischke.de/datenbank/fotos/info_sozialnetz.jpg

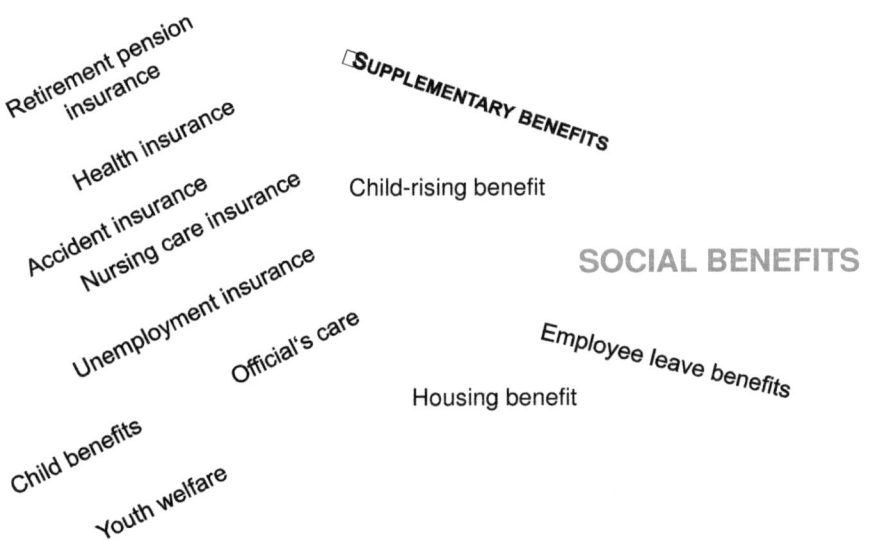

Retirement pension insurance

SUPPLEMENTARY BENEFITS

Health insurance

Child-rising benefit

Accident insurance

Nursing care insurance

SOCIAL BENEFITS

Unemployment insurance

Employee leave benefits

Official's care

Housing benefit

Child benefits

Youth welfare

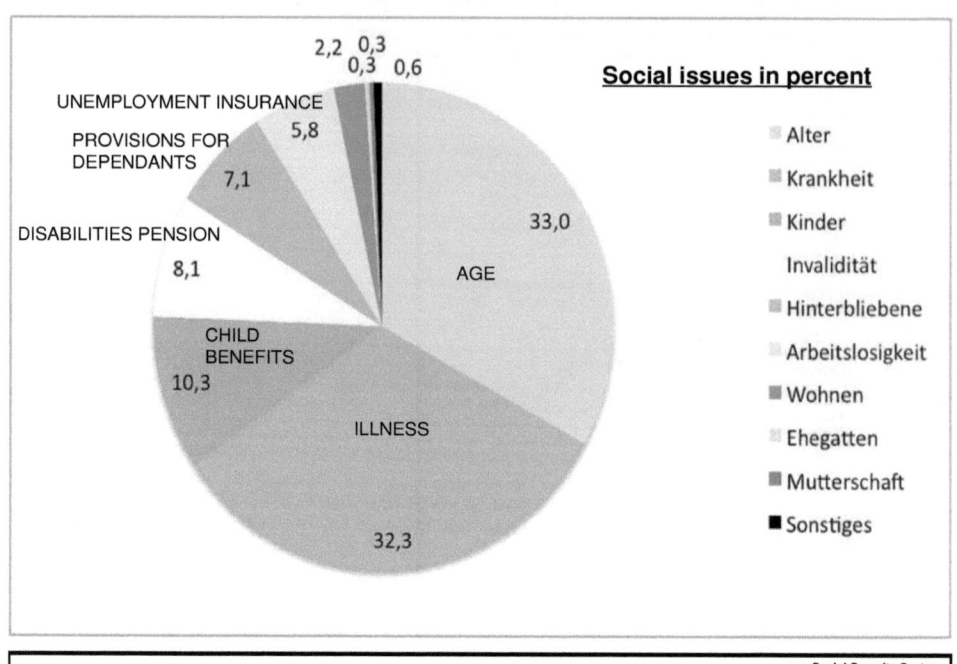

2.2

THE SOCIAL SECURITY

WHAT IS YOUR UNDERSTANDING OF

SOCIAL SECURITY

AND WHICH BRANCHES OF THEM

DO YOU KNOW?

BRANCHES OF SOCIAL SECURITY

LEGAL

HEALTH INSURANCE
RETIREMENT PENSION INSURANCE
UNEMPLOYMENT INSURANCE
LEGAL ACCIDENT INSURANCE

AND

LONG TERM CARE INSURANCE (NURSING CARE)

SOCIAL SECURITY CONTRIBUTIONS

BASIC PRINCIPLE:
Employee 50%
Employer 50%

EXCEPTIONS:
HEALTH INSURANCE,
ADDITIONAL CONTRIBUTION FOR EMPLOYEES

LEGAL ACCIDENT INSURANCE,
Employer 100%

SOCIAL SECURITY CONTRIBUTIONS
2015

AN = Employee
AG = Employer

Health insurance	(14,6%, AN: 7,30%, AG.: 7,30%)
	plus indiviual contributions
Retirement pension insurance	(18,7%, AN: 9,35%, AG: 9,35%)
Unemployment insurance	(3,0%, AN: 1,50%, AG: 1,50%)
Legal accident insurance	(Employer pays alone after risk group)
Long term care insurance	(2,35%, AN: 1,1750%, AG: 1,1750%)

→"CHILDLESS" pays PLUS 0,25% (only employees)

SOCIAL SECURITY

ALL SOCIAL SECURITY AUTHORITIES ARE

BODIES OF THE PUBLIC RIGHT
(WITH SELF-GOVERNMENT)

WHAT IS THE MEANING OF THIS?

SOCIAL SECURITY

BODIES OF THE PUBLIC RIGHT
(WITH SELF-GOVERNMENT)

- ARE AUTHORITIES FOR THE PURPOSES OF THE SOCIAL CODE (INDIRECT STATE MANAGEMENT)

- HAVE MEMBERS (ASSURED)

- ARE FINANCED BY CONTRIBUTIONS (PUBLIC DELIVERIES LIKE TAXES)

LEGAL HEALTH INSURANCE

DO YOU KNOW

LEGAL HEALTH INSURANCE SCHEMES IN GERMANY

AND WHICH PERSONAL GROUPS

ARE INSURED?

LEGAL HEALTH INSURANCE

LEGAL HEALTH INSURANCE

DUTIES

SOCIAL DUTY
- **HEALTH OF THE INSURED PERSONS**
- **EQUALITY OF THE INSURANCE COVER (HOWEVER: ELECTORAL RATES)**

BENEFITS
- **ACHIEVEMENTS**
- **PREVENTION OF ILLNESSES**
- **EARLY DIAGNOSIS OF ILLNESSES**
- **TREATMENT OF ILLNESSES**
- **ACHIEVEMENTS WITH PREGNANCY AND MATERNITY**

LONG TIME CARE INSURANCE

IS ORGANIZED WITH HEALTH INSURANCE SCHEME, BUT SEPARATED (MONEY) MANAGEMENT

DUTIES
DECREASE OF THE FINANCIAL LOADS WITH NURSING NEED

BENEFITS

- **AMBULANT AND**
- **STATIONARY MAINTAINS**
- **DIFFERENTLY ACCORDING TO GRAVITY OF THE ILLNESS**

NURSING STEP (0-3), DELIBERATE ANEW: NURSING DEGREES 0-4

RETIREMENT PENSION INSURANCE

DUTIES

- **REHABILITATION**

- **PENSIONS TO INSURED PERSONS AND MEMBERS**
  - **BECAUSE OF DECREASED CAPACITY TO WORK**
  - **AT THE AGE**
  - **IN DEATH**

    [THE HEIGHT OF THE PENSION DEPENDS BASICALLY AFTER THE HEIGHT OF THE PAID CONTRIBUTIONS AND DURATION OF THE MEMBERSHIP]

- **PAYMENT OF CONTRIBUTIONS (E.G., IN HEALTH INSURANCE SCHEME)**

- **CONSULTATION AND CLARIFICATION**

RETIREMENT PENSION INSURANCE

BEARER

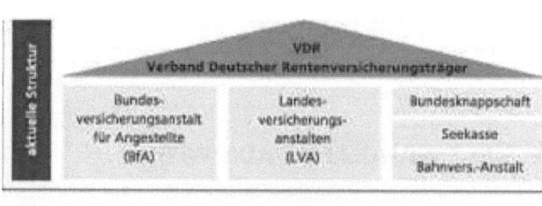
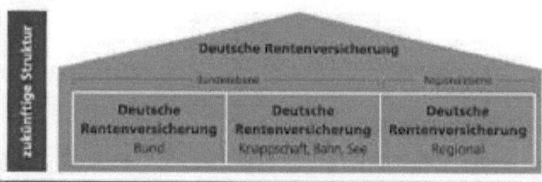

Source: http://pub.mezzo-mac.de/school/image002.jpg

UNEMPLOYMENT INSURANCE

DUTIES:

- **EMPLOYER'S CONSULTATION**

- **MEDIATION IN EDUCATION AND PLACES ARBEITS INCL. CAREERS GUIDANCE**

- **SUPPORT**
  - OF THE PROFESSIONAL TRAINING AND PROFESSIONAL CONTINUING EDUCATION
  - OF THE PROFESSIONAL INTEGRATION OF HANDICAPPED PEOPLE (PARTICIPATES)

- **PRESERVATION AND CREATION OF JOBS**

- **PAYMENT OF E.G., UNEMPLOYMENT BENEFIT**

UNEMPLOYMENT INSURANCE

BEARER:

FEDERAL AGENCY FOR WORK
(BUNDESAGENTUR FÜR ARBEIT)

-REGIONAL MANAGEMENTS

-AGENCIES FOR WORK

-OFFICES

LEGAL ACCIDENT INSURANCE

DUTIES:

DUTIES:

- **ACCIDENT PREVENTION**
  - DECREE OF ACCIDENT PREVENTION REGULATIONS
  - SUPERVISION BY TECHNICAL ATTENDANTS

- **ACHIEVEMENTS WITH CONSEQUENCES OF AN ACCIDENT**
  (WORK ACCIDENT, ROAD ACCIDENT, OCCUPATIONAL DISEASE)
  - REMEDIAL TREATMENT
  - INJURED MONEY
  - ACHIEVEMENTS TO THERE PARTICIPATES AM WORKING LIFE
  - TRANSITIONAL MONEY
  - INJURED PENSION
  - FUNERAL BENEFIT
  - SURVIVOR'S PENSION
  - COMPENSATIONS

LEGAL ACCIDENT INSURANCE

BEARER:

**-PROFESSIONAL
ASSOCIATIONS FOR
DIFFERENT BRANCHES OF
INDUSTRIES, E.G.,
CONSTRUCTION, TRADE,
MINING, TRAFFIC**

**-CIVIL SERVICE, E.G. IN
THE STATE OF BERLIN**

2.3

THE ISSUES OF SOCIAL PROTECTION

ISSUES OF SOCIAL PROTECTION

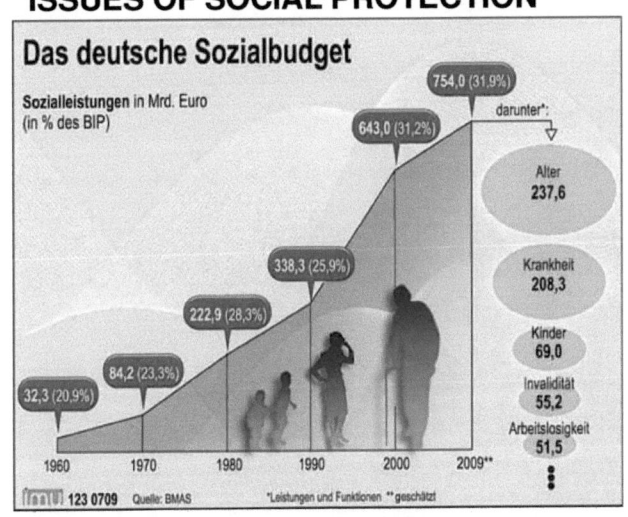

THEREFORE
APPROX. EVERY
THIRD EUR IS USED
IN GERMANY FOR
SOCIAL BENEFITS.

Source: http://www.aerzteblatt.de/bilder/2009/11/img141244.jpg

ISSUES OF SOCIAL PROTECTION

WHAT COULD BE THE REASON

FOR RUNNING RISING

SOCIAL EXPENSES?

ISSUES OF SOCIAL PROTECTION

SOCIAL REPORT

- FOR MANY YEARS RISING PORTION IN EXPENDITURES FOR SOCIAL BENEFITS (SOCIAL BENEFIT RATE), APPROX. 30%

- BAD ECONOMIC SITUATION CAUSED HIGHER SOCIAL EXPENSES

- NO TURN BACK TO THE DEVELOPMENT RECOGNIZABLY

ISSUES OF SOCIAL PROTECTION

SOCIAL WELFARE

IN CASE OF MORE EXACT CONSIDERATION
YOU CAN SEE THAT THE ISSUES FOR SOCIAL WELFARE
TAKES THE STRONGEST RISE AT LAST YEARS.

HOW DOES THIS CONSIST?

Social Security System
Andreas Manthey-Aznavuryan, Professor
at Haybusak University

SOCIAL WELFARE

ANNUAL ISSUES, 2009

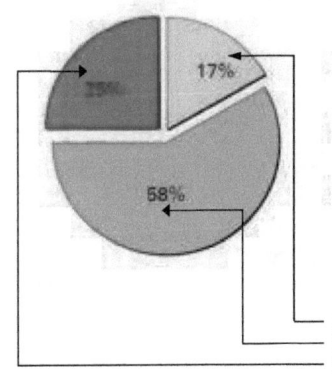

17%

58%

ADDITIONAL HELPS IN NURSING CARE
INDIVIDUAL CASE SUPPORT
OTHER HELPS

BERLIN:
ANNUAL ISSUES FROM APPROX.
1,400,000,000 EUR

ACHIEVEMENT RECEIVER APPROX.
20,000

AVERAGE AGE APPROX.
55.0 YEARS

Social Security System
Andreas Manthey-Aznavuryan, Professor
at Haybusak University

ISSUES SOCIAL WELFARE

SOURCE: OFFICE FOR STATISTIK BERLIN-BRANDENBURG, 2009

E.G., BERLIN

Berlin Social Welfare, 2009	Beneficiary	Issues in EUR
Achievements after 5. to the 9th chapter SGB XII (sum)	53,111	1,403,769,000
of it hepls for health	246	3,412,000
of it integration help to handicapped people	22,900	585,340,000
Of it additional helps for nursing care	25,775	323,156,000
of it help for overcoming more specially more socially – difficulties and help in other situations	5,835	43,299,000

Social Security System
Andreas Manthey-Aznavuryan, Professor
at Haybusak University

SOCIAL WELFARE

BERLIN:

THIRD-HIGHEST ISSUES IN SOCIAL WELFARE ALL OVER THE STATES OF GERMANY

Source: http://bilder1.n-tv.de/img/incoming/crop477088/9589306301-clmg_4_3-w680/SOZIALHILFE-AUSGABEN-4C-JPG-GRA102.jpg

Social Security System
Andreas Manthey-Aznavuryan, Professor
at Haybusak University

ISSUES OF SOCIAL BENEFITS (GENERALLY)

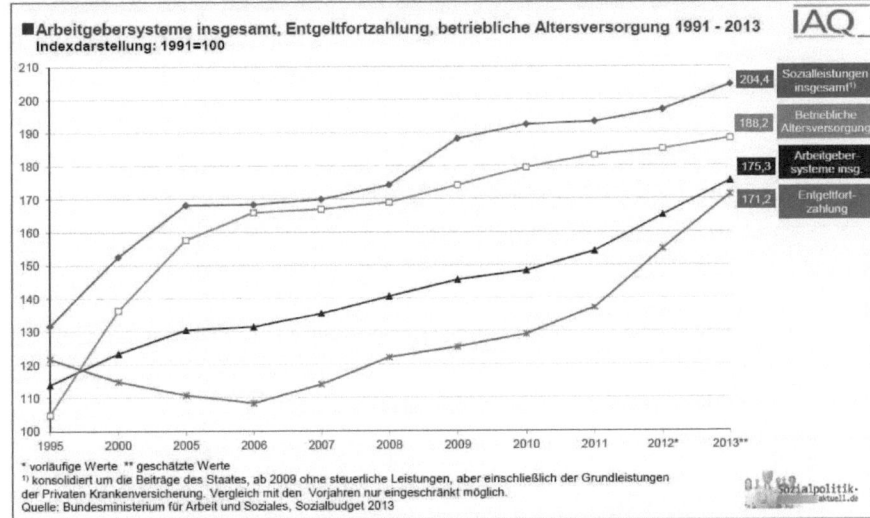

■ Arbeitgebersysteme insgesamt, Entgeltfortzahlung, betriebliche Altersversorgung 1991 - 2013
Indexdarstellung: 1991=100

* vorläufige Werte ** geschätzte Werte
[1] konsolidiert um die Beiträge des Staates, ab 2009 ohne steuerliche Leistungen, aber einschließlich der Grundleistungen der Privaten Krankenversicherung. Vergleich mit den Vorjahren nur eingeschränkt möglich.
Quelle: Bundesministerium für Arbeit und Soziales, Sozialbudget 2013

Source: http://www.sozialpolitik-aktuell.de/tl_files/sozialpolitik-aktuell/_Politikfelder/Finanzierung/Datensammlung/PDF-Dateien/abbII24.pdf

Social Security System
Andreas Manthey-Aznavuryan, Professor
at Haybusak University

ISSUES OF SOCIAL SECURITY

PROBLEM: MONEY GAP

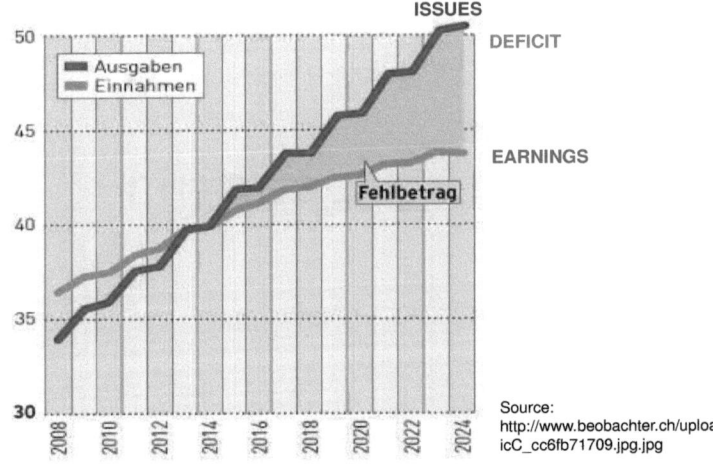

ISSUES

DEFICIT

EARNINGS

Source:
http://www.beobachter.ch/uploads/RTEmag
icC_cc6fb71709.jpg.jpg

Social Security System
Andreas Manthey-Aznavuryan, Professor
at Haybusak University

ISSUES OF SOCIAL SECURITY

WHICH POSSIBILITIES YOU SEE
TO SOLVE THIS PROBLEM?

KEYWORDS:
MORE MONEY TO THE SYSTEM? BUT HOW?
BENEFIT CUT?

2.4

FINANCING OF SOCIAL BENEFITS

FINANCING
OF SOCIAL BENEFITS

<u>FINANCING:</u>

- STATE [FEDERAL STATE, STATES, MUNICIPALITIES]
- ENTERPRISES (CONTRIBUTIONS, TAXES)
- PRIVATE INDIVIDUALS (CONTRIBUTIONS, TAXES)

<u>But:</u>
- Issues of the state for social benefits are raised to the most by taxes of the private individuals before.
- Enterprises have included her issues also before in the price with.

2.5

THREE COLUMNS THEORY

THREE COLUMNS THEORY

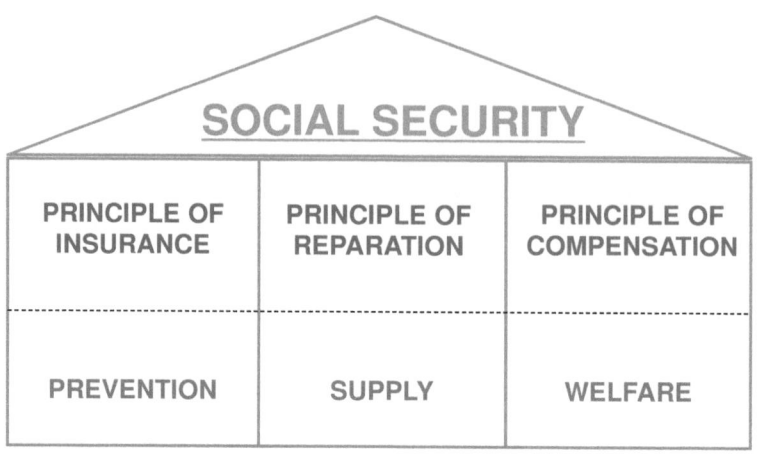

PRINCIPLE OF INSURANCE	**PRINCIPLE OF REPARATION**	**PRINCIPLE OF COMPENSATION**
PREVENTION	SUPPLY	WELFARE

Social Security System
Andreas Manthey-Aznavuryan, Professor
at Haybusak University

THREE COLUMNS THEORY

PRINCIPLE OF INSURANCE	**PRINCIPLE OF REPARATION**	**PRINCIPLE OF COMPENSATION**
HEALTH INSURANCE	**CHILD BENEFIT**	**WELFARE**
	HOUSING BENEFIT	**YOUTH WELFARE**
RETIRMENT PENSION INSURANCE	**OFFICIAL BENEFIT**	**SOCIAL REHABILITATION**
LEGAL ACCIDENT INSURANCE	**WAR VICTIM BENFITS**	
INEMPLOYMENT INSURANCE		

Social Security System
Andreas Manthey-Aznavuryan, Professor
at Haybusak University

THREE COLUMNS THEORY

<u>BUT THERE IS ALSO:</u>

„4. COLUMN"
named

P R I V A T E
PREVENTION

<u>2.6</u>

<u>Duties and objectives</u>

<u>of the social code</u>

DUTIES AND OBJECTIVES
OF SOCIAL CODE

12 books (SGB = Social Law Book)

SGB I   **General part** (valid from 01/01/1976)

SGB II **Basic financial security for unemployment (**valid from 01/01/2005)

SGB III **Promotion of employment** (valid from 01/01/1998)

SGB IV **Common regulations of Social security** (valid from 07/01/1977)

SGB V **Legal health insurance** (valid from 01/01/1989)

SGB VI **Legal old age insurance** (valid from 01/01/1992)

SGB VII **Legal accident insurance** (valid from 01/01/1997)

SGB VIII Child and youth services act (valid from 01/01/1991)

SGB IX **Rehabilitat./Paricitipates of handic. Peopl.** (valid from 01/07/2001)

SGB X **Administrative procedures, Protection of social data,**
                Cooperation of the benefit bearer (valid from 01/01/1981)

SGB XI **Legal long time nursing care** (valid from 01/01/1995)

SGB XII Social Welfare (valid from 01/01/2005)

DUTIES AND OBJECTIVES
OF SOCIAL CODE

HOW IT WORKS?

INSURED PERSON

- **pays contributions, even if no achievements are needed (every month from income)**
- **makes an application for benefits in case of need**

AUTHORITY

- takes the money from the insured persons and distributes them to those which need benefits (no profits)
- checks the application and decides on it (legal claim)

DUTIES AND OBJECTIVES
OF SOCIAL CODE

ON WHICH BASIS THE AUTHORITY DECIDES?

LAW   (e.g., Social Code)

GUIDELINE   (e.g., Health Insurance: from „Joint Federal Committee")

LAW COMMENTARY

AGREEMENTS

JURISDICTION OF THE HIGHER SOCIAL COURTS   (like Law)

DUTIES AND OBJECTIVES
OF SOCIAL CODE

AND WHAT IF I WILL NOT AGREE WITH
THE DECISION OF THE AUTHORITY?

DUTIES AND OBJECTIVES
OF SOCIAL CODE

This is also regulated!

- ABOUT EVERY APPLICATION IS A WRITTEN ANSWER GIVEN

- IN THIS ANSWER IS CONTAINED A LEGAL REMEDY INSTRUCTION (IST A MUST!)
  - → LAW STATE PRINCIPLE

DUTIES AND OBJECTIVES
OF SOCIAL CODE

IF YOU NOT AGREE WITH THE ANSWER THERE IS THE FOLLOWING PROCEDURE POSSIBLE:

- INSERT CONTRADICTION AGAINST THE ANSWER
  - The authority has to proof the decision about the new arguments
  - If the authority remedy the answer it gives a new anser with another legal remedy contradiction
  - If the authority cannot remedy the contradiction, it remits a written contradiction answer

- COMPLAINT AT THE SOCIAL COURT
  - Against this contradiction answer only complaint can be inserted at the social court within one month

SOCIAL COURT AFFAIRS

3 INSTANCES:

First: **SOCIAL COURT**

→ For a district ... e.g., Social Court of Berlin

→ They proof alls decisions of the social authorities

Second: **HIGHER SOCIAL COURT**

→ For one or more States ... e.g., Higher Social Court for the states of Berlin and Brandenburg

→ They proof the decisions of the social courts

Third: **FEDERAL SOCIAL COURT**

→ They proof the decisions of the Higher social courts

SOCIAL COURT AFFAIRS

SOCIAL COURT

→ Chambers

→ 3 judges (1 professional, 2 honorary judges)

HIGHER SOCIAL COURT

→ Senates

→ 5 judges (3 professional, 2 honorary judges)

FEDERAL SOCIAL COURT

→ Senates

→ 5 judges (3 professional, 2 honorary judges)

LEGISLATIVE PROCEDURE

GERMAN LEGISLATION

HOW IS A FEDERAL SOCIAL LAW MADE?

FIRST ONCE THERE ORIGINATES THE IDEA.
- FROM THE GOVERNMENT,
- FROM THE MINISTRY,
- FROM REPRESENTATIVES,
- FROM THE BUNDESRAT (STATE'S CHAMBER),
- ON TIP OF A FEDERAL COURT
- OR ON ACCOUNT OF A PETITION OF A CITIZEN

...

GERMAN LEGISLATION

STEPS (short version)

1. The first draught of the law goes to the Bundestag (Federal Parliament).

2. This gives it to the responsible committee of the parliament.

GERMAN LEGISLATION

3. The committee consults on it, take a hearing to experts and delivers a recommendation.

4. Then goes the law with the recommendation to the plenary sitting of the parliament.

GERMAN LEGISLATION

5. The parliament goes for the vote.
If the law finds the majority, it is decided. If not – return to Step 3 (max. two times).

6. Because it is a federal law, the state's chamber cannot decide on it.

7. Signing the law by the Federal President.

EUROPEAN UNION

European Social Charter (ESC)

EUROPEAN UNION

European Social Charter (ESC)

October 18th, 1961,
valid from February 23rd, 1965
19 Social rights

Last update:
May 3rd, 1996,
valid from July 1th, 1999
31 Social rights

EUROPEAN UNION

THE EXERCISE OF SOCIAL RIGHTS
HAS TO GO WITHOUT DISCRIMINATION
FOR REASONS

- OF THE RACE,
- THE SKIN COLOUR,
- OF THE GENDER,
- THE RELIGION,
- THE POLITICAL OPINION,
- THE NATIONAL DESCENT OR
- THE SOCIAL ORIGIN

BE GUARANTEED.

EUROPEAN UNION

SOCIAL RIGHTS

(Election)
...

11. Everyone has the right to benefit from any measures enabling him to enjoy the highest possible standard of health attainable.

12. All workers and their dependents have the right to social security.

13. Anyone without adequate resources has the right to social and medical assistance.

14. Everyone has the right to benefit from social welfare services.

...

EUROPEAN UNION

SOCIAL RIGHTS

...

15. Disabled persons have the right to vocational training, rehabilitation and resettlement, whatever the origin and nature of their disability.

16. The family as a fundamental unit of society has the right to appropriate social, legal and economic protection to ensure its full development.

17. Mothers and children, irrespective of marital status and family relations, have the right to appropriate social and economic protection.

...

EUROPEAN UNION

SOCIAL RIGHTS

E.G. Health

Article 3 – The right to safe and healthy working conditions

With a view to ensuring the effective exercise of the right to safe and healthy working conditions, the Contracting Parties undertake:

1.to issue safety and health regulations;

2. to provide for the enforcement of such regulations by measures of supervision;

3. to consult, as appropriate, employers' and workers' organisations on measures intended to improve industrial safety and health.

...

EUROPEAN UNION

SOCIAL SECURITY

... AND...

EVERY INSURED PERSON CAN GO TO ANOTHER STATE TO TAKE BENEFITS

BUT: IT ALWAYS BINDING THE LAW OF THE MEMBER STATE WHICH I TAKE UP THE SERVICES

PLUS: BILATERAL AGREEMENTS BETWEEN STATES OUTSIDE THE E.U.
(E.G. GERMAN-TURKISH AGREEMENT ABOUT SOCIAL SECURITY

NATIONAL OFFICE FOR SOCIAL SECURITY IN EVERY MEMBER STATE

...

EUROPEAN UNION

SOCIAL RIGHTS

E.G., HEALTH INSURANCE CARD (German version)

Source: https://www.aok.de/medien/baden-wuerttemberg/form/eGK_vorder_rueck_aok%20bw.jpg

---

EUROPEAN UNION

SOCIAL RIGHTS

E.G., HEALTH INSURANCE CARD (Italian version)

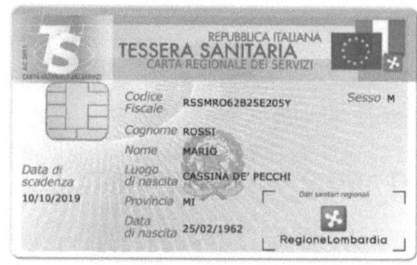 

Source: http://www.comune.ripaltacremasca.cr.it/public/upload/image/2013/Layout%20TS-CNS%20scadenza%202019_OK.jpg
http://assistenza.finanze.it/knowledgebases/puntofisco/image/GestioneUtenti/tessera.gif

GROUP WORK 1

YOU GOT THE ORDER TO BUILD UP IN YOUR COUNTRY A HEALTH INSURANCE ARE BASED WHICH INSURES OF ALL PEOPLE.

IN WHICH STEPS WOULD YOU GO FORWARD AND WHICH BENEFITS SHOULD THE HEALTH INSURANCE AT LEAST CONTAINS?

PLEASE, DISCUSS YOUR IDEAS WITHIN THE GROUP AND PRESENT YOUR SOLUTIONS.

GROUP WORK 2

NOW YOU KNOW THE GERMAN SOCIAL SECURITY SYSTEM. PLEASE, CHANGE YOUR PERSPECTIVE NOW.

WHAT YOU HAVE TO DO, SO THAT THE SYSTEM OF THE SOCIAL PROTECTION FUNCTIONS IN GERMANY NOT FURTHER AND BREAKS SOMETIME?

PLEASE, DISCUSS YOUR IDEAS WITHIN THE GROUP AND PRESENT YOUR SOLUTIONS.

GROUP WORK 3

GERMANY HAS A VERY GOOD SOCIAL SYSTEM AT INTERNATIONAL LEVEL. STILL THERE ARE MANY PROBLEMS WITHIN THE SYSTEM. IS ITEVEN MORE DIFFICULTLY GROWING FINANCING OR THE PROBLEMS OF THE GENERATIONS BECOMING OLDER. ALSO MANY PEOPLE ARE LIVING AS A SINGLE, NOT IN FAMILY LIKE BEFORE.

WHAT WOULD YOU DO, SO THE SYSTEM FURTHER FUNCTIONS ON A CONTINUING BASIS? WHICH STEPS WOULD YOU ADVISE?

PLEASE, DISCUSS YOUR „PER" AND „AGAINST" WITHIN THE GROUP AND PRESENT YOUR SOLUTIONS.

THANK YOU

FOR YOUR ATTENTION!

ALL THE BEST AND A LOT OF SUCCESS!

YOUR KNOWLEDGE HAS VALUE

- We will publish your bachelor's and master's thesis, essays and papers

- Your own eBook and book - sold worldwide in all relevant shops

- Earn money with each sale

Upload your text at www.GRIN.com and publish for free